Experience Antique Booth Success

A Step-by-Step Guide on How to Run an Antique Booth Efficiently

Copyright © 2014 by Retro Aficionado

All rights reserved. No part of this publication may be reproduced, distributed, or transmitted in any form or by any means, including photocopying, recording, or other electronic or mechanical methods, without the prior written permission of the publisher, except in the case of brief quotations embodied in critical reviews and certain other noncommercial uses permitted by copyright law.

Disclaimer

This book is designed to provide information on how to run an antique booth only. This information is provided and sold with the knowledge that the publisher and author do not offer any legal or other professional advice. In the case of a need for any such expertise consult with the appropriate professional. This book does not contain all information available on the subject. This book has not been created to be specific to any individual's or organizations' situation or needs. Every effort has been made to make this book as accurate as possible. However, there may be typographical and or content errors. Therefore, this book should serve only as a general guide and not as the ultimate source of subject information. This book contains information that might be dated and is intended only to educate and entertain. The author and publisher shall have no liability or responsibility to any person or entity regarding any loss or damage incurred, or alleged to have been incurred, directly or indirectly, by the information contained in this book. You hereby agree to be bound by this disclaimer or you may return this book within the guarantee time period for a full refund.

Table of Contents

Introduction **5**

Chapter One: Run the Booth as a Business **7**
- *Familiarize Yourself with the Antique Booth Industry* *7*
- *Use Your Passion to Create a Business Vision* *8*
- *Maximize the Benefits & Anticipate the Challenges* *9*

Chapter Two: Locate the Best Market **11**
- *Find the Best Antique Mall* *11*
- *Source the Funds & Make a Budget* *12*
- *Supply the Demand & Fill Your Inventory* *14*

Chapter Three: Manage the Booth **15**
- *Set up a Standout Booth* *15*
- *Get the Word Out & the Customers In* *16*
- *Build Relationships & Networks* *17*

Chapter Four: Debunk the Myths and Know the Facts **18**
- *Myth vs. Fact: You can only sell antiques* *18*
- *Myth vs. Fact: You can manage on your own* *18*
- *Myth vs. Fact: You can be firm on prices* *19*

Chapter Five: Know the Best Practices & Common Errors in the Business **20**
- *Dos* *20*
- *Curate & Diversify with Best Sellers* *20*
- *Rearrange & Update Your Booth* *20*
- *Maintain Security* *21*
- *Don'ts* *21*
- *Settle for Breaking Even* *21*
- *Hoard & Panic Buy* *22*
- *Under and Overprice Your Items* *22*

Chapter Six: What's Next? **24**

Conclusion **25**

Introduction

The antique booth industry is a highly lucrative business, not only because of its potential for profit but also because it is a natural extension to every collector's dream of amassing new items and thrill of finding hidden treasures.

This book is the ultimate guide for beginner and experienced antique booth owners who want to make it out in the industry. It provides you with a step-by-step guide on how to transition from being a collector to a successful antique booth owner.

This book is for you if:

You are new to the business and do not know where to start. It contains straightforward and practical steps from knowing the basics of the industry to building your inventory, from locating the best antique mall to making a standout booth and from acquiring new collections to pricing them at competitive prices.

You are experienced and want to improve your business methods. It shares with you the many dos and don'ts of veterans in the business with decades of experience. It also updates you with the recent trends in the business, such as staging, using technology and social media to advertise your booth with minimal or no extra cost.

You are apprehensive about the cost of the business. It gives you the current market rates for the ideal capital investment and expenses such as rent, commissions and other miscellaneous costs.

You do not have a collection yet and would like to start one. It tells you where to find the best deals for building on your inventory through auctions, sales and networks.

You are worried because of the confusing information you find. It debunks myths on the industry with hard facts that you can use to your advantage.

Begin and run your antique booth business now!

Thanks again for downloading this book, I hope you enjoy it!

Chapter One: Run the Booth as a Business

In this chapter you will learn:

- The past, present and future of the business
- The development of your business' vision
- The pros and cons of the business

Familiarize Yourself with the Antique Booth Industry

As the value of money and other properties fluctuate, savvy investors are looking into alternative ways to store the worth they have accumulated. Along with the popularity of television shows that entice viewers with the possibility of finding an obscure but rare item in the market, consumers and investors today are flocking in search of the next big find, and they look for these hidden treasures in antique booths.

Antique shops have been in business for hundreds of years, and while it used to be the hobby of rich collectors, aristocrats and the nobility, today the average person has an equal opportunity of finding these much sought-after items through antique booths.

In the recent past, antique booths have become a popular destination for these avid collectors and a whole industry of malls has been set up just for the booth business. Most states in the US will have an antique mall and business is booming.

The idea behind this partnership is that every person can set up an antique booth, either with their own collection, from buying and reselling at a profit, or both. Previously, fairs or other events allowed these booths to be set up on roads or empty plots of land. The daily setting up and taking down of the booths made malls a welcome alternative. Today the booth and the antiques are protected from the elements and business owners have more access to a larger customer base.

Whether driven by investing, collecting or just plain curiosity, there's an established market for antiques, and while the demand increases, supplies may not be able to meet them. After all, genuine antiques are not manufactured and are only one of a kind. Starting an antique booth is easier said than done and managing it and making it profitable for you are entirely different things. One thing is for sure though, antique booths are here to stay and the opportunity is too hard to resist.

Use Your Passion to Create a Business Vision

Almost all antique dealers begin as collectors and most of the time it starts as a curiosity, a hobby, an obsession and finally blooms into a lucrative business. Regardless of how it started, they all began with a sense of motivation and passion.

If you're a beginner then make sure that antiques and vintage items are your passion. You will need this kind of motivation to push you towards the challenges that you'll face in the business and, when you do, you will definitely reap the rewards.

Create your merchandise from items that you are truly interested in; it could be inspired by a cherished childhood memory, a specific decade or genre that you always reminisce about or unique and niche items that will tickle anyone's curiosity. Let your passion for these items be your guide in creating a business out of your collection.

You can choose from three business models for antique booths and you can use these to either start or manage your business:

1. Sell your own collection
2. Buy and sell other collections for a profit
3. Combination of the two

What is it about antique booths that make you feel most passionate? Is it the chance to get money out of it? Then business model one may the best for you. Are you interested in the thrill of treasure hunting from auctions, open houses, garage sales or pawnshops and then reselling them for a profit? Then business model two may be your choice. If you have your own collection and want to travel and amass more antiques, then a combination of both could be the perfect match for you.

Maximize the Benefits & Anticipate the Challenges

If you're a collector then an antique booth is one of the best pairs for your hobby. It presents several benefits aside from just money and profits. You can show off your collection not only to buyers but also to your peers. You gain access to a bigger family or network of collectors who you may not otherwise know if you stayed at home. You get to see other people's antique items and collections. You also get to share each unique story behind every piece in your collection.

However, your ideal world of a community of collectors is inside a real and practical world. To be part of that world, you need to pay rent, set up a booth, market your merchandise, have customers and, although not as important as taking pride in your collection, you have to earn profit.

In every business there is a risk and antique booths have challenges too. You must anticipate these problems before they occur to make your booth run as smoothly and efficiently as possible. Some challenges include poor profits, limited or mismatched merchandise, low number of customers and the security of your collection.

Your best solution to these challenges is knowledge. Remember, as a collector, you should have an above average and almost expert level of knowledge with the merchandise you are selling. This information is the highlight of your booth, aside from the actual item. How old is it? Where did it come from? What's it for? What is it made of? How many are there? How much were they before and what is their value now? These are some of the questions that you have to be able to answer at a moment's notice. Do your research over the Internet, visit antique auctions, malls and shops or ask other collectors to gain a better understanding of the value and potential of your collection.

If you are a collector first and a business owner second, you must know some basic business skills first. You need to know about price ranges, customer care, advertisements, budgeting, inventory and other skills to help not only run but also manage your booth.

You do not need a degree in business management for your booth, what you need is enough working knowledge to help you with the first few months of your business and after that experience will take over as your teacher.

Chapter Two: Locate the Best Market

In this chapter you will learn:

- The best location for your booth
- The income and expenses of your business
- The alternative sources of your merchandise

Find the Best Antique Mall

The antique mall can make or break your booth. There are several criteria to help you make the best choice:

1. Location
2. Popularity and Credibility
3. Rent and commission rates
4. Policies, manpower and management

Location, location, location; this is one of the most important criteria for your booth. The best malls should be right in the middle of town and along a busy road. Make sure the mall will have enough parking spaces, especially if your merchandise is larger in size. If you can find a mall that is adjacent to other popular businesses, that will be an added bonus. Don't be worried that there are other antique malls near the area, instead of competition, think of it as a potential for attracting other antique buyers to your booth.

Think of location in terms of how it will affect you as the business owner. If you plan for this to be only a sideline, then you have to choose a mall that is as close to your office as possible. If you plan to devote all your time to it, then consider a mall that is near to your home.

Research the name of the antique mall and find the reviews or feedbacks from customers, booth owners and other collectors. If a mall has a bad reputation of hosting fake or knock off antiques, then it will harm your booth. Even if a booth is distinct from the mall, chances are customers will associate that mall with your own booth. Make sure you choose good company in your business; their reputation will rub off on you as a booth owner.

Malls generally have the same terms for all antique booth owners. If you are new to the mall, you will be required to sign a six-month lease. After that period, you can rent the space on a monthly basis. Rent is calculated on a per square foot basis. On top of that, malls require you to pay a commission for merchandise you sell. A low rent may mean a mall does not get as much traffic as a more expensive mall. Make sure you get the price for these expenses before you commit.

Rates range from two to ten dollars per square feet and get more expensive depending on the mall's location. Commission rates range from five to twenty percent. Some malls only require you to provide the items and they will do the selling for you, other malls will ask you to assist them. Other things you have to check include mall policies on insurance, discounts and licensing.

Aside from the mall itself, you must also consider the actual space for your booth.
Some malls have dead areas that customers skip, especially the corners and second floors. Get a space that is closest to the start and end of the mall and closest to the cashier.

Source the Funds & Make a Budget

Every business venture will require some form of capitalization. Fortunately, in the antique booth business, chances are you already have amassed enough items to build your inventory. If not consider using funds that you saved for investment activities as money to stock up on your merchandise. The ideal investment will be around five hundred to two thousand dollars. Remember, the antique booth does not require a large amount of funds to start; you can begin with small sales and profit margins and gradually build on your nest money.

As soon as you have your funds, make a budget of your expected expenses and set a target income that will net you with a desirable but realistic profit margin. Aside from rent and commission expenses, you should anticipate other expenses. Most malls will only have spaces and will not provide tables, cabinets, chairs or fixtures to set your merchandise. The best option is to bring, or recycle, any unused furniture you may have at your house to your booth to save on cost. Make sure that these items match the overall look of your space.

Other miscellaneous expenses may be supplies and materials for your booth. Take into account gasoline expenses as you travel to and from the booth or to different sources of antiques that you can resell. It is important to take into account all of these expenses so you can create an accurate target profit.

An excellent way of guaranteeing profit is to have a minimum of ten to fifteen percent markup on any item that you are selling. This is meant to cover not only the value of the merchandise but also the overhead expenses of the antique booth.

There will be business owners who are only in it for the thrill of the sale and the company of people who share their interests. If this is the case, profit is not that much of an issue for them and they will be satisfied if they can just cover the rent and other overhead expenses. On the other hand, if you are interested in not only the hobby but also the profit, you have to be very conscious of how much you spend and earn. Set realistic targets, especially in your first month and then gradually increase your profit margins, as you get better at it.

Supply the Demand & Fill Your Inventory

Although you will start with your own collection, it is important that you also meet the demands and interests of your customers. Use their interests as your guide as you fill out your inventory. For example, if you notice that there is a high demand for silverware, then on your next run to the auction you have a shopping list of what to buy. If you notice that your customer base in your neighborhood are richer and have more money to spend, then highlight or choose antiques that are more upscale.

You should also be open to people who walk into your booth with the intention of selling instead of buying. It is important to decline from buying, especially if you have no way of guaranteeing authenticity and actual value of the item. If you start with a small purchase from these walk-in sellers, chances are they will return and keep on trying to sell you some of their items. Say "no" all the time except, of course, when you find a good and authentic deal.

Aside from your own collection, you can also source your stock from auctions, flea markets, thrift stores and garage or estate sales. You can find out when and where these sales events occur from your peers, the mall owner and on the Internet. Once you reach the event, remember two principles: buy low and diversify. Fill your booth with items that you bought at a reasonable price. Resist the temptation to pay more than the actual value of the item; chances are you might not be able recoup the investment.

When you have established yourself in the business then that is the time to take more business risks. Consider renting additional space, buying more expensive antiques and becoming an authority on a specific genre of antiques that you will exclusively sell.

Chapter Three: Manage the Booth

In this chapter you will learn:

- The tips to make your booth stand out
- The marketing strategies to attract customers
- The relationships and networks you need

Set up a Standout Booth

If you rented the standard ten by fifteen square foot booth, then you should always have this dimension in mind whenever you plan to move your collections from home or your purchases from an auction. Even if you find a good deal, your booth may not have the space you need to sell your merchandise and you will resort to storing it in your house.

Aside from making sure your inventory fits in your space, how to arrange it is another opportunity to improve your sales. Instead of lining up your items, like in a conventional store, you can stage your booth. In booth staging, you can create an area as if it is a scene from your collection's origins. For example, if you have a 1950s collection of spoons, knives, cups and plates, instead of stacking similar items together, set up a dinner table in your booth. Create a dinner table setting complete with an antique table, linens, centerpiece, and napkins and, of course, price tags. The scene will entice customers not only to look at your setting but also increase the potential of having them buy the entire set.

Instead of neon bulbs, you can also use antique lights to change the mood of your booth. Instead of a huge table filled with your inventory that is between you and your customers, make a walkway inside your booth that will allow your customers to come in and browse and touch your items. Instead of just sales talk, play music that's appropriate for the era of your antiques. If there are empty walls on the sides of your booth, hang pictures and other antique items that you can install to make a cohesive look. Remember to put in accents such as flowers and other bursts of colors to make your booth more interesting.

Make sure you have a balance between decoration and functionality. Your design may look nice but without enough items to interest people, customers may just pass up on it.

Make sure that, even before you move your collection to your shop, all items are properly inventoried, cleaned and priced. Use paper price tags and strings that you can loop around your items. Keep your supplies both in your house and your booth just in case you need them.

Get the Word Out & the Customers In

Most antique malls will cover the advertisement of your booth through signs outside; this advertisement is insufficient. You have to take control of your own marketing strategy to increase the chances for success. Post flyers in your local town hall, bulletin board and other conspicuous places to get the word out about your booth. Ask family and friends to tell others about your booth.

Take advantage of social media and various business platforms that are available over the Internet. Ask for help if you are not familiar with how to set up Internet accounts, but in the long run you should be able to do the advertising yourself.

Consider taking pictures of your booth and items and then publishing them over the Internet. You can create a Facebook or an Instagram account to advertise your collection, tag friends and link it with a map of your booth. You can also create an eBay account if you want to create virtual access to your booth.

If you are a savvy computer user, consider writing a blog about your collection. Write short and interesting articles about each item with pictures. Ask your customers to post comments or feedback on your blog. Link your blog to antique club websites and multiply your reach.

Remember to link a Google map to your Internet accounts; it will give your potential customers better directions than just copy pasting the address of the antique mall. Make an email dedicated to your antique booth business so you can create a means of communication.

Build Relationships & Networks

You have to take care of and commit to building relationships with your customers. Regardless of their background or interest in your booth, greet and invite them to your shop. Entertain their questions and do your best to answer all of them. Do not be afraid of saying that you do not know the answer instead of making up a story. Thank them for visiting whether they buy an item or not. If they are looking for something that you do not have, tell them you will be on the lookout for that item. Remember to tell them when you will have new inventory or when you plan to have a sale.

Avoid doing other things when you are in the booth. Talking with someone on the phone or chatting with another over a laptop will just discourage your customers. You must also know how to assess a potential customer; some prefer to have your complete attention while they shop, while others would prefer that you maintain at a distance as they browse.

Aside from your customers, you also need to create a network of your peers. Maintain a professional relationship with your mall owner; you may get the best space in the mall on your next lease. Your auctioneers may give you a heads up on their next event and give you a sneak peek at their items. You can even benefit from building a relationship with your peers. They can refer their own customers to you if you have what they need. Make sure you return the favor.

Chapter Four: Debunk the Myths and Know the Facts

Myth vs. Fact: You can only sell antiques

Technically, before an item can be called an antique, it must be at least a hundred years old. Only cars are exception to this rule, they need at least twenty-five years to be called an antique. Aside from age, other characteristics include condition, rarity, quality and beauty. If you have genuine antiques in your collection, then they can be part of your antique booth.

Each mall will have their own policy on what can be sold on their spaces; some will be very strict with their inventory, while most are more lenient with the 100-year rule. This is because items in antique malls are bought not only for their age and other technical characteristics but also because of the personal connection with customers.

Antique malls will host the sale of vintage, collectible and rare items even if they are not antiques. This means, that whether you actually have hundred-year-old items or not, your collection will most probably be allowed in the antique mall.

Myth vs. Fact: You can manage on your own

The ideal scenario is that you have all the time in the world to manage your own booth, however, in the real world there are few people who can devote their entire day to their booths. Some have day jobs or other commitments; some can only visit during the weekends or at certain hours of the day. Hiring someone will just reduce your profits. If this is the case then you may need help. Antique mall owners know these sorts of problems and they have made solutions for them.

Some antique malls will have in house personnel to manage the booth and sales for you. Some even provide a service of calling you whenever there is a very interested customer who asks for a discount. You can even brief mall employees on your items for sale so they will be able to answer queries from your customers.

Still, you must make time to visit your own booth and look after your own inventory. When you do, make the most of it. Check for anything broken and report it immediately, if an item is missing, most likely a customer picked it up and just moved it elsewhere when they lost interest. Review the sales and find out which items are the best sellers and make the appropriate adjustments in your inventory.

Myth vs. Fact: You can be firm on prices

You may have calculated for an airtight budget and made accurate markups on your prices but chances are people will haggle. Most antique malls and booth owners allow negotiation on prices. Discounts are part of the antique business and you need to know your limits. If you want to be firm on your prices while other booths beside you negotiate, then it may hurt your sales.

If you do give out discounts, make sure to choose wisely. It's best to negotiate with your regular customers instead of those who rarely visit your booth. As long as you are within the markup price range, you can use discounts to your advantage. It will show your customers that you value their patronage and they will be encouraged to become regulars.

Chapter Five: Know the Best Practices & Common Errors in the Business

Dos

Curate & Diversify with Best Sellers

Make sure you have a variety of antiques that you can sell. Your customers will come from different backgrounds and each will have their own interests. Instead of focusing on a very specific type, diversify your merchandise. Consider small and big pieces, high and low end items, antiques from Europe, Asia and other cultures. The more variety you have, the more interesting your booth becomes and the more customers will visit you. The best sellers include:

1. Glassware, ceramics, pottery and metal crafts
2. Dolls and toys
3. 1950s home decoration
4. Dining flatware and plates
5. Military antiques

Rearrange & Update Your Booth

As you acquire new antiques to sell, make sure to change your booth to match your new collection. Use your new merchandise as an opportunity to attract more customers. Nothing entices customers more to window shop than new items. Constantly changing your booth gives the impression that your booth is experiencing more sales. Another advantage is that you can secretly tuck in old items that were not sold before into the new collection.

Watch out also how others change their booths and make sure you do something to make yours stand out. Consider hanging a sign with a catchy name for your booth. Give out business cards to customers.

Maintain Security

Although the security of your items is the mall's responsibility, it is still best to look after your own interests. Some security measures you can use are showcases. These are glass cabinets with locks that can store valuable antiques in your inventory. You can opt to make special arrangements with the mall owner for securing these items. Most antique malls will have secure storage for high-end items.

One of the best ways is to choose a space that is as close to the mall security personnel as possible. If you have the funds, consider adding a security camera on top of the mall's own. Every bit of deterrence against theft will be needed with high value antiques.

Don'ts

Settle for Breaking Even

If you are in the antique booth activity just for the thrill of it, then breaking even may be a good result for you. However, if you approach it as a business, then you must not settle for just covering the overhead expenses. You must be able to reward yourself not only with the collecting, hunting and networking but also with money.

If you always just break even, chances are you'll not be able to sustain your antique booth. You also may not acquire more items to build on your inventory. You may even lose motivation if you use money outside of the antique booth business to cover up for its losses.

Losses are bound to occur but if they happen regularly, you may consider moving to another mall. You may have the right items and the right prices but not the right place. Most experienced antique booth owners change malls when they see a pattern of losses.

Hoard & Panic Buy

If you see a deal in an auction, do not be tempted to immediately buy it. Take into consideration your booth space. If it won't fit and you would have to store it either in your house or leave it for longer periods of time in your booth then you are already losing money. The longer it takes to turnaround on an investment the more money you stand to lose. This is because you will use up your booth space for other items that could have been sold much earlier. Another reason is that you have already spent the money that would have been used for other items that have better chances of selling.

Always give yourself limits on how much of your collection will be stored in your house. There is a tendency to hoard collections and wait for the time your booth space clears up for other items. As much as possible, do not let your collection take over your home, especially if you share your house with others.

Under and Overprice Your Items

It is important to know the market prices for the items you have. Unless it is absolutely rare or one of a kind, chances are you can find something that is either exactly the same or similar to your collection. When in doubt on the price, you can do your own research on the exact value.

You can ask your trusted peers and even expert customers what the value of the item is. You can go to auctioneers and appraisers to get a better idea. For especially difficult items, you can try to contact museums or historians for a better grasp of the collection.

There is a curious pricing strategy that experienced booth owners swear is effective. Although it may seem counterintuitive, pricing a low value item high may give it better chances of being purchased than pricing a high value item low. This is because consumers today associate price with value. The more expensive the item, the more valuable they perceive it. Think about this strategy in your pricing decisions.

Remember, values and prices are not necessarily the same. It is up to you to determine the price that you will need to put on an item to sell it. Take into account not only value but also the overhead expenses you have to pay for and the target margin you have to meet.

Chapter Six: What's Next?

Now that you have a solid foundation for the antique booth business, the next step is to put your knowledge to work. Remember to take small steps first, especially if you are a new in the business.

Go to your collection now and start an inventory, it will be best if you can have a thorough list of items that include description, date acquired and date made, and even better if you have a story or progeny. Next choose only the items that you are one hundred percent sure you can part with. Do not cheat yourself by saying you will buy back what you have already placed in your booth.

If you are an experienced antique booth owner, then use the tips in this book to refine and improve your business. Open a dedicated social media account for your booth and publish it as soon as you can.

Regardless of your level of experience in the antique booth industry, it is important for you to know that it takes more than a collection to make your booth a success. You need to run it as efficiently and wisely as possible, with the steps and tips listed in this book, to make your antique booth prosper.

Conclusion

I hope this book was able to help you to learn the steps in starting and running your antique booth. I hope you have gained sufficient working knowledge in starting your first inventory or you have improved your current antique booth.

If you enjoyed this book, then I'd like to ask you for a favor, would you be kind enough to leave a comment and review for this book on Amazon.com? It'd be greatly appreciated!

Finally, if you ever happen to find yourself in Gilroy, CA please feel free to visit my antique booth.

Retro Aficionado, Booth #21
Collective Past
7495 Monterey Street
Gilroy, CA 95020

Good luck!

Made in the USA
Middletown, DE
07 January 2017